SUPER SIMPLE

HANGING GARDENS

A KID'S GUIDE TO GARDENING

ALEX KUSKOWSKI

Super Sandcastle

An Imprint of Abdo Publishing
www.abdopublishing.com

Consulting Editor, Diane Craig,
M.A./Reading Specialist

www.abdopublishing.com

Published by Abdo Publishing, a division of ABDO, PO Box 398166, Minneapolis, Minnesota 55439. Copyright © 2015 by Abdo Consulting Group, Inc. International copyrights reserved in all countries. No part of this book may be reproduced in any form without written permission from the publisher. Super SandCastle™ is a trademark and logo of Abdo Publishing.

Printed in the United States of America, North Mankato, Minnesota
102014
012015

Editor: Liz Salzmann
Content Developer: Alex Kuskowski
Cover and Interior Design and Production: Mighty Media, Inc.
Photo Credits: Jen Schoeller, Shutterstock

Library of Congress Cataloging-in-Publication Data

Kuskowski, Alex.
  Super simple hanging gardens : a kid's guide to gardening / Alex Kuskowski.
     pages cm. -- (Super simple gardening)
  ISBN 978-1-62403-523-4
1. Hanging plants--Juvenile literature. 2. Container gardening--Juvenile literature. I. Title. II. Series: Kuskowski, Alex. Super simple gardening.
  SB432.5.K87 2015
  635.9'65--dc23
                          2014023974

Super SandCastle™ books are created by a team of professional educators, reading specialists, and content developers around five essential components—phonemic awareness, phonics, vocabulary, text comprehension, and fluency—to assist young readers as they develop reading skills and strategies and increase their general knowledge. All books are written, reviewed, and leveled for guided reading, early reading intervention, and Accelerated Reader® programs for use in shared, guided, and independent reading and writing activities to support a balanced approach to literacy instruction.

TO ADULT HELPERS

. . . .

Gardening is a lifelong skill. It is fun and simple to learn. There are a few things to remember to keep kids safe. Gardening requires commitment. Help your children stay dedicated to watering and caring for their plants. Some activities in this book recommend adult supervision. Some use sharp tools. Be sure to review the activities before starting and be ready to assist your budding gardeners when necessary.

. . . .

Key Symbols

In this book you may see these symbols. Here is what they mean.

Sharp!
You will be working with a sharp object. Get help.

Inside Light
Put your plant inside.
Direct Light = in sunlight.
Indirect Light = in shade.

TABLE OF CONTENTS

Get into Gardening 4

Hanging Gardens. 5

Ready, Set, Hang! 6

Tools 8

Safety 9

Dig into Dirt. 10

Pick Your Plants 11

Location Station. 12

Plant Doctor 13

Cool Care. 14

Plant Pocket 16

Flip-a-Plant 20

Up in Knots 24

Plants On Air 28

Glossary. 32

GET INTO GARDENING

Gardens don't have to be in the ground. Or in pots. Plants can still surround you. You can make a hanging garden!

It is easy to start. This book will give you simple tips. Explore the world of gardening. Get your hands dirty. Grow something great!

HANGING GARDENS

· ·

Hanging gardens are easy to create. Grow flowers upside down. Get a plant to float on air. Make a plant hanger with knotted rope.

READY, SET, HANG!

Before you hang your plants, check that it is safe! Make sure that what you hang your plant on can hold the weight. Test any hooks before hanging plants on them.

Watering

Make sure you can water your plants regularly! Take each plant off its hook. Place it in the sink. Water it. Let it sit for 1 hour. Hang the plant back up.

Plant Tip

Set a watering **schedule**. Check the soil to see if your plant needs water. Stick a finger into the soil ½ inch (1.3 cm). If it is dry, the plant may need water.

TOOLS

These are some of the important gardening tools you will be using for the projects in this book.

containers & pots

garden gloves

hand trowel

plants

soil

rocks

watering can

moss

SAFETY

Be safe and responsible while gardening. There are a few rules for doing gardening projects.

Ask Permission

Get **permission** to do a project. You might want to use tools or things around the house. Ask first!

Be Safe

Get help from an adult when using sharp tools or moving something heavy.

Clean Up

Clean up your working area when you are finished. Put everything away.

DIG INTO DIRT

Most hanging plants need soil to grow in. It gives them **nutrients**. Keep your hanging plants healthy by using the right soil.

Choose the best soil for your plants. If you don't know, ask a gardener for help.

Desert Potting Mix
This soil works best with **cacti** and other **succulents**.

All-Purpose Potting Mix
This soil works well with most plants in pots. Buy soil with **peat moss** and **vermiculite**.

PICK YOUR PLANTS

· · · · · · · · · ·

Pick the right hanging plants for you! Many plants make great hanging plants. Try ferns, spider plants, ivy, and philodendrons.

LOCATION STATION

Find a Spot

Hang plants in a place where they can soak up the sunlight! Find out exactly how much sunlight your plants need.

Pick a Pot

Choose lightweight **containers** for your hanging plants. Make sure to use the right size for each plant.

TIP

If a hanging pot has a hole in the bottom, cover it with rocks or **mesh**. That will keep soil from falling out!

Use the Right Size Pot

Plants need room to grow! The roots should not touch the sides of the pot.

Small Pots

Pots less than 8 inches (20 cm) deep.

Medium Pots

Pots 8 inches (20 cm) to 16 inches (40.5 cm) deep.

Large Pots

Pots deeper than 16 inches (40.5 cm).

COOL CARE

Watering Wisdom

Plants need water. Keep the soil moist for most plants. If the soil feels dry, water your plants!

Fertilizer

Fertilizer is food for plants! Most plants need fertilizer every few weeks. The package will tell you how much to use.

The Right Light

Light is important! Get the right light for your plants. Check how many hours of sunlight your plants need.

Get the right light for your hanging plants. Notice where the light comes from. If you hang your plant on a wall, south facing walls get the most light. North facing walls have the least light.

PLANT DOCTOR

Take care of your hanging plants. Check on them often! Follow this list to make sure they stay healthy.

- Pull off dead leaves and flowers.

- Cut off any unwanted leaves with a sharp scissors.

- Check for bugs. Learn about any bugs you find. Find out if they are good or bad for the plant.

PLANT POCKET

COLOR YOUR ROOM WITH PLANTS!

INSIDE
INDIRECT SUN

Supplies
• • • • • • • • •

air dry clay,
purple & green

ruler

teaspoon

wooden skewer

cord

scissors

potting soil

spider plant

garden gloves

sealant spray

DIRECTIONS

1. Mix the purple and green clay together. Twist the colors together.

2. Roll the clay into a ball about 3 inches (7.6 cm) wide. Smooth out any lines or cracks.

3. Use the teaspoon to scoop out a hole in the clay. Even out the walls with your fingers. Make the walls ¼ inch (.6 cm) thick.

Project continues on the next page

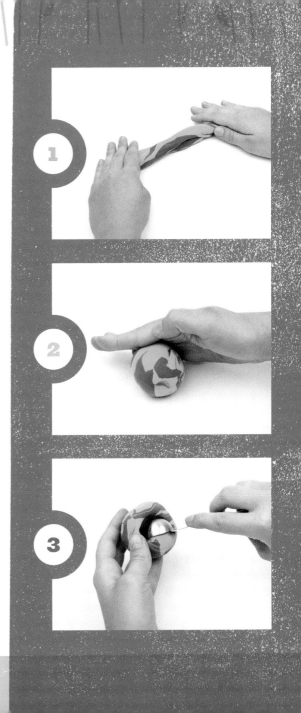

4 Poke a hole on each side of the planter. Make the holes ¼ inch (.6 cm) from the edge. Let the clay dry. Spray with sealant spray. Let dry for 24 hours.

5 Cut a piece of cord 12 inches (30 cm) long. Tie a knot at one end.

6 Push the cord through one of the holes. Go from the inside of the planter to the outside.

7 Push the cord through the other hole. Go from the outside of the planter to the inside.

8 Tie a knot in the end of the cord.

9 Put a little potting soil in the planter.

10 Stick the bottom of the spider plant in the dirt. Hang up the plant!

COOL CARE

Hang the plant in a sunny room. Water the plant every other day over a sink.

19

FLIP-A-PLANT

GROW A PLANT UPSIDE DOWN!

Supplies

• • • • • • • • •

newspaper
plastic yogurt container
craft knife
ruler
Mod Podge
foam brush
glitter
scissors
cord
craft foam
pen
petunia seedling
potting soil
hand trowel
garden gloves

CAUTION SHARP!

INSIDE INDIRECT SUN

DIRECTIONS

1. Cover your work area with newspaper. Have an adult make a small hole on each side of the **container**.

2. Draw a circle 1½ inches (3.8 cm) wide on the bottom the container. Have an adult cut out the circle.

3. Cover the sides of the container with Mod Podge.

Project continues on the next page

4 Sprinkle glitter over the Mod Podge. Let the glue dry.

5 Cut a piece of cord 36 inches (91 cm) long.

6 Push the cord through both holes in the **container**. Tie the ends together.

7 Trace the bottom of the container on the foam. Cut out the circle. Then cut to the middle of the circle. Cut a ½-inch (1.3 cm) hole in the middle.

8. Take the plant out of its tray. Pull gently at the roots to loosen them. Place the foam circle around the plant near the roots.

9. Carefully push the top of the plant through the hole in the **container**.

10. Add potting soil. Fill the container to 2 inches (5 cm) from the top.

11. Water the top of the container over a sink. Hang up the plant by the cord.

COOL CARE

Hang the plant in an area with low sun. Water it every 2 to 3 days over a sink if the soil is dry.

UP IN KNOTS

PUT ANY POT UP IN THE AIR!

INSIDE INDIRECT SUN

Supplies

· · · · · · · · ·

English ivy seeding

garden gloves

ceramic pot,
5 inches (12.7 cm)
wide by 4 inches
(10.2 cm) tall

potting soil

hand trowel

cotton cord, light
blue & dark blue

scissors

ruler

3-inch (7.6 cm)
metal ring

DIRECTIONS

- - - - - - - - - - - - - - - - - -

1 Take the plant out of its tray. Pull gently at the roots to loosen them.

2 Place the plant in the pot. Add soil. Press down gently. Make the soil firm.

3 Cut two light blue and two dark blue cords 48 inches (122 cm) long.

- - - - - - - - - - - - - - - - - -

Project continues on the next page

4 Slide the ring to the middle of the cords. Fold the cords around the ring.

5 Make a loop in the cords. Put the ring through the loop. Pull to tighten. The knot should be right next to the ring.

6 Group the cords into pairs. Each pair should have a cord of each color.

7 Tie each pair of cords in a knot. Make the knots 7 inches (18 cm) from the ring.

8 Make four new pairs. Each pair should have cords of the same color.

9 Tie a knot in each pair of cords. Make the knots 5 inches (12.7 cm) from the **previous** knots.

10 Measure down 3 inches (10 cm). Tie all the cords together in a knot.

11 Put the pot in the hanger. The pot should rest on the final knot.

COOL CARE Hang the plant out of direct light. Place a bucket under the ivy while watering.

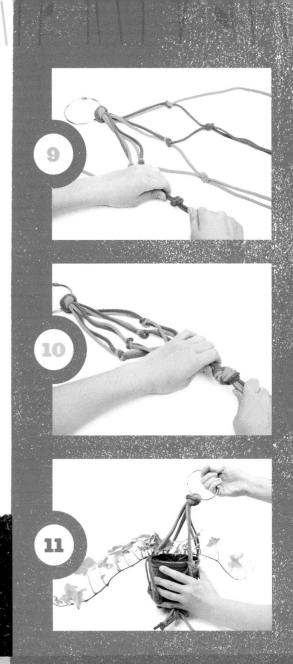

PLANTS ON AIR

THESE PLANTS SEEM TO FLOAT!

Supplies

- small twig nest
- plastic wrap
- twist ties
- ruler
- garden gloves
- hand trowel
- potting soil
- small fern seedling
- moss
- rocks
- raffia
- scissors
- 3-inch (7.6 cm) metal ring

INSIDE INDIRECT SUN

DIRECTIONS

1 Line the nest with plastic wrap.

2 Use twist ties to hold the plastic wrap in place. Push a twist tie through the edge of the plastic wrap and around a twig. Twist ends of the twist tie together. Put a twist tie every 2 inches (5 cm) around the nest.

3 Put potting soil in the nest. Cover the plastic wrap.

4 Take the seedling out of its tray. Pull gently at the roots to loosen them.

Project continues on the next page

5 Dig a small hole in the dirt. Put the seedling in the hole.

6 Fill dirt around the seedling. Pat the soil to make it firm.

7 Put moss around the seedling.

8 Cover the rest of the soil with rocks.

9 Cut twelve pieces of raffia 30 inches (76 cm) long. Separate the raffia into four groups of three strands.

10 Thread a group of raffia strands halfway through the twigs on one side of the nest.

11 Thread the other three groups of raffia strands through the nest. Space the groups evenly around the nest.

12 Tie the strands together above the fern.

13 Separate the strands into two groups. Tie them together around the metal ring. Cut off any extra raffia.

COOL CARE
Hang the plant in indirect light.
Check the plant every 2 to 3 days.
Water the plant over a sink.

GLOSSARY

cactus – a plant with sharp spikes instead of leaves that grows in hot dry places.

container – something that other things can be put into.

fertilizer – something used to make plants grow better in soil.

mesh – a sheet made of threads or wires woven loosely so there is space between them.

nutrient – something that helps living things grow. Vitamins, minerals, and proteins are nutrients.

peat moss – a type of moss that usually grows on wet land and is used in gardening.

permission – when a person in charge says it's okay to do something.

previous – the one or ones before.

schedule – a list of the times when things will happen.

succulent – a plant, such as a cactus or an aloe, that has thick stems or leaves that store water.

vermiculite – a light material that holds water that is often added to potting soil.